SUE STEWART

Inventing the Fishes

ANVIL PRESS POETRY

Published in 1993
by Anvil Press Poetry Ltd
69 King George Street London SE10 8PX

Copyright © Sue Stewart 1993

This book is published
with financial assistance from
The Arts Council

Designed and composed by Anvil
Photoset in Bembo by Wordstream
Printed and bound in England
by Morganprint Blackheath Ltd

ISBN 0 85646 248 9

A catalogue record for this book
is available from the British Library

Flying fish on page 69 by Jo Fairfax

For John

ACKNOWLEDGEMENTS

Acknowledgements are due to the editors of the following magazines and other publications in which some of these poems first appeared: *Acumen, Ambit, Grand Piano, Illuminations, The Independent, London Magazine, Orbis, Other Poetry, Oxford Poetry, Poetry Matters, Poetry Review, Prospice, Resurgence, South West Review, Strawberry Fare, The Times Literary Supplement* and *Women's Review*. Other poems were included in prose contributions to *Delighting the Heart: A Notebook by Women Writers* and *Taking Reality by Surprise: Writing for Pleasure and Publication* (The Women's Press), and in poetry anthologies *Compass* (Headland Publications), *Four Ways* (Phoenix Press) and the *Blue Nose Poets Poetry Anthology*. 'Inside Wolf' was one of six finalists in the TLS Cheltenham Poetry Competition 1988, 'Any Other Way' won first prize in the Rhyme Revival Competition 1988, and 'Mother of Pearl' won fifth prize in the Peterloo Poets Open Poetry Competition 1991. 'You Ask for Secrecy' was read on the TVS programme *This Way Out*.

The 'Book of Hours' poems were illustrated by Celia Ward, and an exhibition of the poems and illustrations was shown at the Poetry Society and the Maas Gallery, London. The 'Genesis' sequence is part of a new collaboration with Celia Ward.

My thanks to writer Adam Thorpe for his critical and sensitive help in arranging the manuscript.

CONTENTS

When	9
Match Girl	11
Bluebells	12
Serendipity	13
Dust	14
The Muse Comes to Call	15
Fair Weather	17
From 'Book of Hours'	
4 am	19
11 am	20
2 pm	21
4 pm	22
5 pm	23
8 pm	24
9 pm	25
11 pm	26
Midnight	27
November	28
Too Many Cooks	29
Sibyl	30
Mother of Pearl	31
Stepping Stones	33
Apple	34
Testing the Water	35
You Ask For Secrecy	36
Hope	37
Greater Spotted	38
From 'Genesis'	
Light	39
The Wind	40
Moon	41
Dividing the Waters	42
Inventing the Fishes	44

The First Acorn	45
Eggshell	46
Feathers	47
Butterfly Chapter	48
Grass, Bramble, Herb	49
The First Poppy	50
Cattle, Beasts and Creeping Things	51
Snake	52
Wood, Stone, Sand, Clay	53
Snail-Woman	54
Beached Dogfish	55
Any Other Way	56
Nature Walk	57
Catherine	58
Feeling the Cold	59
Cinders	60
Sleeping On	61
Hansel's Birthday	62
Inside Wolf	63
Persephone	64
Lucinda's Act	66
Bookend	67

WHEN

When you know you must change
you look back at the leaves
like a shadow, inventing reasons
for staying small.

When you know you must change
trees skate past the window of your train
and the fields' pages spell out your itinerary.
It is simple as a stamen's antenna.

When you know you must change
you make silence your convent,
pure and sharp as salt. The bricks
pile up like little lies, impishly.

When you know you must change
you walk in several directions all at once.
The sky instructs you in the art of cleansing.
Cloudy letters remain unanswered.

When you know you must change
you meet the intermediary in a buttonless coat.
You can't read her face but her words spill out
like a flock of bats. You do everything she says.

When you know you must change
you are unprepared, caught like a moth
in the act of leaving.
Your dusty wings sprout freckles, pinpricks.

When you know you must change
you move furniture on the fourth day,

as if the violet darkness were not
a regular visitor. She breathes herself
behind the curtain, stays very still.

When you know you must change
a hundred frowns assemble on the horizon,
each bearing a different grudge.
You rub them out, one by one.

When you know you must change
the room suddenly seems warmer.
An owl flutes in the forest.
An answering call trembles up your throat.

MATCH GIRL

Know me by the swan's jaw, by the rasp
of a box that's as long as the season.
I'm stiff as a board in its communal bed.
Angles keep me dry, like a cough going inward.
Bits of me peel off in splintery threads.

Sometimes the bed tilts and I try to spill out
like a pencil. Other times I shuffle forward,
at one with the others, fatalistic and mellow.
Shall I brand a cigarette its setting sun,
make newsprint shiver into moony peaks?

Fingers reason with us, lift the chosen one.
I look the other way, fill up the hollow,
hold my flame in a bubble of blown glass.
Darkness muffles its scalding curve,
the bed shifts back in its pithy slide.

A noise up the wall, like paper being ripped.
Then a flare, a hiss, a blue whisper fading.
A spent smell darkens our fellowship.

I lie low, isolated by thought,
phosphorus head defying sleep.

BLUEBELLS

The bluebells have other ideas
waking limp from their pointed dream,
the analysis of vases.

Their ragged tint is more telling
than the restless prose I wrap them in,
comforting each one
as I snip its sticky fuse

stretching the flora like fingertips
to the east and west of windows,
frayed lips easing down
to kiss the sill.

They crave the teapot,
a larger pool to lean from
where tannin homely as loam
fosters their lilac sheaf

my kitchen's bulb
warming the surface
as a sun might.

SERENDIPITY

> *Alalcomeneus was the first man to appear, by Lake*
> *Copais in Boeotia, before even the Moon was.*
> – ROBERT GRAVES

You'd be in silk – emerald I think,
its frou-frou as crisp as leaves –
with perfume a ghost at your ears
where copper moons hang like apples,
your foot on the taxi's metallic step

and there he'd be,
burnished, at one with the leather;
best of Earth's fruits, a few
inadequate leaves necklacing his waist –

Alalcomeneus, breezing in from Attica
to celebrate the net result of all his
choices – to step on this leaf not that,
eat the black berry not the red. He thinks
of himself as forked tree, asking for rain.

He makes for the moons, believing them
to be his own, for weren't there whispers
at his death-bed? 'Moon', they murmured,
as if delivering a kiss, 'There will be Moon'.

Pavements fade with a thousand cries.
Moons tumble in the green silk of your lap
where he, wonderingly, looses them
and you fall to your knees like Athene
for knowledge, his own rough tutelage.

DUST

Into the empty spaces comes Wednesday
offering itself like a virgin,
as if I didn't know how to please
or as if the sky had fallen in,
showering me with kisses.

I peel a wet petal from the bark,
let the rain drum its future into me.
It tells longings like beads, Ariadne
sliding through them in knots.

Her necklace is private as a fan,
to be cast aground with other common things.
One day you will taste it in leaf
or in the not-quite-ready autumn plums,
the dust on their purple sheen
like the gathering of souls.

THE MUSE COMES TO CALL

I'm at the door
more alive than ever
thinking myself thin
like a genie before
the liquid dive

and it's through the keyhole,
ballooning on the other side,
heady on the sweet air of rooms
that have seen me before.

I've run amok in your
bed of roses, now I tip up
the table your elbows seem
bent on depressing

and steady your hand, the one
you tried to feed me with
and place it to your lips,
hushing them from
their own idea of themselves.

I'm in your palm
sliding down the lifeline
weightless, evading the ambush
of your curious eye

in your skull
trying out for size
the length and breadth
of the thoughts you wear

needling for change,
the pleat and tuck
of a tailored phrase.

I'm in your pulse
driving at a theme
your pen my baton

conducting me to the cliff
of your chalky page
and just at the brink

I come into my own
sprinkling a few grains
on the sea of your poem.

FAIR WEATHER

On the day of ice I am the plaintiff
at the bench, making lists with a wounder's art.
You are stopped in mid-sentence with no defence.

On the day of snow I adopt a child's tread,
trying to please. Lit windows tilt their squares on me
like false flags. How many people drink to my emptiness?

On the day of thaw I betray all my indiscretions.
The sound of tea pouring is a confidante's question.
As I lift the cup, liquid thinks out loud.

On the day of chill I walk under laburnum arches.
They tempt me with their pockets of coins.
Quickening my pace, I enter the bee's drunken sleep.

On the day of rain I let fall the ruby ambition.
Bark seethes like a nest of snakes, testing.
On the ground, a mulch of stricken leaves.

On the day of frost I invent the meaning of teeth.
Nibbled to nothing, I uncover a bandage of leaves.
How many flames does it take to eat the sad air?

On the day of drought I pay the final taskmaster.
I am his devoted student, laying a table
of parched cornstalks. They rest, unfinished flutes.

On the day of cloud I am a sheet ghosting the line.
My flapping panics are bleached into wanness.
Blushing at the thought, you recover your position.

On the day of lightning I have aimed a matron's scissors.
They slide through grey silk, precise and attentive.
Like a scorpion, they pine in the doing.

On the day of thunder I reiterate the sacred laws.
They bounce off the walls, checking me with echoes.
I have come of age, and startle my own sister.

On the day of fire I consume the bronze hours.
The stubborn veins I save till the last.
What skeleton now robs me of sleep?

On the day of hail I batter you with unearthed sadnesses.
They are hard with hurt and will not have the door
shut against them. Let them fall.

A carpet of marbles unsteadies my step.
I become weightless.

From 'BOOK OF HOURS'

4 A.M.

Dawn sneaks through
in slow motion
nudging the clock

four strokes
of a brush
dipped in light

a clearing
like throat
before chorus

Dawn's overnight bag
is a water-colour
left out in the rain

thinning out
the silence

its hem leaves
a trail of frost
vampire teeth

a loop of briar
takes the dew
for a halo

a rustle of silk
in the hedgerow

the birds begin.

11 A.M.

11 a.m. treads water
in a million kettles
waiting for its moment

reflects that window-dressing
is not its business
as it sits level-headed
in plastic or china

or laps confined within sheer banks
the embroidery of occasion
stitched across its piping belly

and it mingles in any company
though a little proprietorial
gushing sympathy in kitchens

or pressing itself upon desks
topped with formica or leather
employing, as the mood dictates,

milk, sweeteners, cigarettes
for the ends
of its discreet fraternity

now wafting by in a heat wave
veiling recipients
in a cinematic focus

softer than neon or bulb
and more pliant than this frank light
searching every room and yawning cupboard
for traces of whim and whimper.

2 P.M.

I advance the afternoon's cause
a trailblazer
on divided territory

I daren't look
at the wistful hours falling away
behind me, but press on in all weathers,
active service my only school

and I am richly rewarded
when I see people's backs
blown by the gale of my mouth

to desk, field or home
one eye on me as they kiss
their lovers goodbye...

I rival all affections
in my commissioned chair
for I rule by fear

and if I'm not revered
I pass the grudge on
to my colleagues

who catch up with the offender
before the day is out.

4 P.M.

Walk the path of my small maze
and you will find me hospitable
baking scones and beating cream
in my shrubby enclosure

making free with
my slice of afternoon
your daily taste
of green seasoning

and though ticking
is my only perennial
I place the windswept cyclamen
like doves at a corner table

to remind me of
my own modest sweep
as I put the scones out to cool
and fetch cups, saucers, plates

favouring no one
in my flat and flowered apron
soon to fold up
in its dusky drawer.

5 P.M.

My reputation precedes me.
You stand when I enter
my chimes your anthem

and follow my drift
a fluorescent wand
pointing you home.

My own outlook is bleak
pinned against an office wall
interfered with from behind
interrogated through glass

but I rest one hand
on my lower back
and wave goodbye
with my godmotherly flair.

I like to muse
on the manner of exit
between bullet and snail

as I release you from contract
into the ampersand of youth,
the evening's fiction.

8 P.M.

The homebody in you
may keep me indoors –
face glazing over

as I count the span
of improbable drama
from a polished screen –

or your night owl,
my flapping escort,
seat me at a friend's table

or in a darkened auditorium
where usherettes fake
the glow-worm's art

but my steely limbs
stretch like a compass
encircling Greenwich,

your latitude and longitude
the warp and weft
of the threadbare slacks

I slip in and out of,
a born tourist
with a knack for leaving.

9 P.M.

On waste land
in a spirit of ambush
I snuff out the flames
of the rose-bay willow

and in country lanes
wrap a widower's scarf
round the Old Man's Beard

but I throw stars
like loose change
on the sky's table

giving with one hand
what I take with the other

sidereal lamps
balancing my dark look

as I balance the books and
tot up constellations –
Plough, Dipper, Orion...

11 P.M.

At my quiet reminder
you relinquish the vertical

untangling your curls
with a sober hairbrush

and drifting to bed with
a dizzy attempt at romance

sometimes forgetting to remove me,
my light tut-tut
on your Cinderella arm

or perhaps you find a book
worth leaving me for,
a paper corner your refuge,

though all pages spell my career
remembering their infancy
in a harness of bark,

the pithy reason
of middle years

and now the shelf-life
where they yellow
like autumn leaves

ageing by the second
my hand on their spines,
the unmarked lacunae.

Midnight

I'm at the window
kissing the hem
I slip beneath

a go-between
to ferry you
to the subliminal bank

drifting the cargo
of your eyelids
over iris moats

or a night thief
rummaging for dreams
in my roomy holdall

colluding with anima
to pull you into
sleep's pocket

then stealing time
as you plummet the face
of my hempen wall.

NOVEMBER

Come the evening I gather my own,
more missed-the-boat than apron.
Liquid the sparrow's late news,
roses ladle the weight of rain.

Weeks back bonfires flicked Jaffa whips
my cat occupied the verb to doze
and poppies stained the corn
with their gift for interruption.

Now beauty cools, distils into shade.
Monkish feathers litter the grass.
You query dry gold, was it ever crisp:
answers slide from a petalled room.

TOO MANY COOKS

My fingers stretch the yeast.
It's fresh and suggestive,
slides down the cup's hill – kitchen's
warm, and the bowl. Hands are cool.

Sugar grains fly like spore,
white on cream. The jug tilts,
its warm water a spilt pool.
In it falls my wooden spoon.

Flour and salt marry:
one is vague, one pragmatic.
Liquid foams at the cup's lip –
flour invites it, yeast carries.

The towel has discretion,
I use it as duvet
while boasting hours pass below.
Dough settles for the bowl's rim.

My punch deflates. I lift
and knead for eight minutes,
forcing in gobbets of air:
plop in a tin, brush with egg.

Poppy seeds hurtle down.
Somewhere in their tight heads
is a harvest, a red past.
I cover them with darkness.

Our dough grows outlandish,
meets the oven's burnt truth
and comes out terracotta –
Vesuvian, fixed in mid-

SIBYL

I moved your violets
to the rockery
tangled as ever

and put out seedlings
to harden off
thinking of you

voice thick with Ulster
fingers weighed in rings
mouth pursed tight
around a cigarette

afraid of loose lips
and pennies on lids
that hangdog look
the last gasp brings.

MOTHER OF PEARL

Yes but I wanted a boy, to be honest.
Her father's stuck on this son and heir routine –
God knows, don't ask. Shells, mainly;
soap-dishes, combs, lampshade stucco, ashtrays.
Positively rococo, tasteless as dead bait.
I humour him – well, you have to, don't you?

I said to her at sixteen, Pearl, you
just forget those bloody Sirens. Be honest,
you're too – well, plump, and pallor's no bait
for a game of sailors. It's the old routine –
you've to set the scene with rum and ashtrays,
low lighting – look available, mainly,

not tight as a clam. Her father's fault, mainly,
planting the itch of malcontent. I tell you
she's either butch in pants, kicking ashtrays
in the fire, playing at 'being honest'
or mooning in June with her mermaid routine.
I keep my cool, refusing to take the bait

or take it just to spit it out, the sexist bait
she dangles above us – at bedtime, mainly.
We're creatures of habit, we like our routine,
you don't want me to spell it out, do you?
She calls our reticence lying, her cheek honest,
then stubs us out like fag-ends in ashtrays,

forgetting the family business is ashtrays,
that tick of sand her world. What a bait
she'd have been, and what a prize! If I'm honest
I had great things in mind. A string, mainly,
a whole chain to grace a lady's neck – you
know the sort of thing, it's quite routine

back there, where it's deeper. A different routine
for us, down-market with seaside regalia, ashtrays
and the like. He works all hours. Well yes you
would understand wouldn't you? We're easy bait.
Now where's my ticket? Last of the cutlery, mainly,
and my blonde wig. This is what comes of 'Ms' Honest.

The whole routine stinks, like rotting bait
or dirty ashtrays. She's misguided, mainly,
and by who? You put her up to it, let's be honest.

STEPPING STONES

The first stone was white and blue.
Traced in the weave of Welcombe Beach
It became a symbol to bind our days.

The second, tossed at your feet
By lazy November wave, bled salt
Like a grey heart on wet boots.

The third stone lay flat as a penny.
Atlantic rub had bruised and seasoned
Its shoulders to young geometry.

Three birthday stones large as oranges
Guard our home where rain is their tide.
White stripes circle their bellies.

The seventh stone is Sarsen.
Kin to time, it anchors a white wall
Watches from a magic eye.

In dream the stones marry.
Belly holds eye, white stripe is cloud.
Sarsen heart mocks granite.

I turn from the sea. Clouds shift
Behind you as you wait
At the cliff-top.

The stones spell my path toward you.
The moon has not yet come.
At last the sea is too bitter to live by.

APPLE

After rain, drips from the roof.
The garden has that rinsed look
and still heavy, skin-soaked
from its shower of wands.

I should have picked the apples,
clinging on into November.
Pools gather round the stalks:
elsewhere, mercurial, dart or drop.

Trees offer their best sides,
wet barks that simulate shadow.
All the edges are smudged.
What houses there are, on the hill,
rub out the horizon.
In the woods a deer coughs.

How clean it all is, and how indifferent.
The cool green apple rests in my palm.
I am a seat for the cool green apple.

TESTING THE WATER

In the shape of a cloud
I'm jostled from Monday to Wednesday, gathering
my thoughts on the wing. Some drift off.
All my life is a training in letting go.

In the shape of the rain
hold my interest and I'll strip your worries
like feathers. They land uncertainly,
making arch suggestions about coracles.

In the shape of a stream
I have swallowed my own name in the rush
to establish an alibi. Now I brush
with death, whose walls are armed against me.

In the shape of a river
my yarn is invisible, unbroken by sleep's scissors.
I follow the letter of the law
and grant small acts of kindness.

In the shape of a waterfall
I fall apart to absolve you.
How long can you defy my coolness?
Ill at ease, I contemplate the horizontal.

In the shape of the sea
I have no eyelids. My ardent wish
is to be caught basking in moonlight.
I take her face and crumple it in a mother's arms.

In the shape of a tear
there is safety in numbers.
I nurse my little grief in a crocheted smock.
Together, we make for the hills.

YOU ASK FOR SECRECY

You ask for secrecy, a poem
that nudges in the dark like a mushroom.
Words dot the page in untidy spore.
Will they swell to its prim balloon,
thumbnail sketch of a stubborn mule?

Half a poem blinks at the light
in slow motion, considering its options.
It's growing fast. Shall I pick at it,
peel back the meaning for a slice of life?
Or enjoy its rawness, the uncurdled bite

of random words? Could it tumble
down your throat and disappear
like a lost flavour of wildness?

The secret's out.
Words mushroom their mumbly poem.

HOPE

For Anne

Heading out to sea, your blue crawl
uncertain as the sky, what a brave fin
you make, interrogating the sun.
Confusion is the tide's invention,
one ripple answering Diana,
another your fingernail's slide.
New love flows better than old love,
one kiss saying I was born to this,
another tasting of salt and wrack.

Limpid dreams are cool as noughts,
offering whirlpools to spin in.
Romance blooms in your eyes, extravagant
as anemones. Husband and sons follow
their own spindrift, as husbands and sons
will; wordless or voluble, angry
or spent. The lighthouse rises
with the glow of planets in his arms,
promising shells, and order, and oysters.

I wish you a salmon horizon,
would heap a pile of finished sentences
in your lap, fed and watered and
taking the bait. But shoals gather
in the underbelly of your stroke,
memories float like buoys, flotsam. This
is an interim poem lacking all conviction,
but as full of hope as you, and he,
lunging like a whale to escape dry land.

GREATER SPOTTED

Woodpecker comes to break bread
swanning in for high table, the
mark of the goddess upon him

waxing lyrical on the rust
gingham of his wiry nut-sac and
crossing out its tawny noughts.

Tail-feathers fan their black and white
crazy-paving spotted with blood. His
top hat slips, breast swells like a

full sail or new-lain egg as he
taps anew at a crust's closed door.
Broody wagtail lands and leaves

out of his depth. Greenfinch and
yellow-hammer throw out complaints
as they head for the woods.

Only the humble sparrow remains,
falling like a pebble on discarded
scraps: flung nuts, flown crumbs.

Humbler still, I hold vigil from an
open window in secret courtship,
knowing the drill.

From 'GENESIS'

Light

It is empty of guile, like water,
and has the gift of flowing
but everything water is, it is not.

It is both master and servant,
returning with a broom to see the night off.
Moths twirl away like sycamore seeds.

It is a lifter of veils,
a painter without easel or brush.
It gives shape, but is shapeless.

It says, 'No, this is curve of eyelash
and this, the straightness of a twig.'
It can't keep secrets, publicises your every look.

It inches its way towards shadows,
confident in the power of vanishing.
They abandon their safe distance.

It is generous, giving its sum total
to all without favour. Its steady glide
is like a thin wash, cleansing and isolate.

It is in at the beginning,
overseeing every leaf and whisker.
Turning your back is no escape.

The Wind

To you I give the gift of speech,
a dozen tempers of the heart,
a penny-whistle's querulous art,
a woman's way to be out of reach.

Why is your face all streaked and torn,
where did you toss the things I said?
When will you nudge the rose's head,
where make a sea of the bed of corn?

Yours is the power to ruffle the deep,
yours is the hand that wields the knife.
Yours the invisible way of life,
yours the forbidden dream of sleep.

Circling a compass, a stranger to death,
running away is your constant aim.
Your name is mischief, is blameless harm.
Your daughter is sweet, a baby's breath.

All things move to your chequered rule,
the blasted tree and the willing scarf.
Deflecting the rain is not enough.
The earth is your playpen and your school.

Moon

She came to me in a dream
like one of those light thin showers
that barely reach the ground
and her beauty was perfectly formed
and she gave only half of herself.

So I fashioned her from half-truths
and the deepest love, delirium
and the material effect of kindness,
and she grew into changeling in my hands,
embodying all the paleness I longed for.

And the paleness is adopted by pearls.
If quietness needed maps they'd be here
and if radiance revealed its agenda
it would be written on her face of snow,
and of second thoughts, and of turning away.

For what is awry she favours most
and all things tilt with her milken list.
You'll follow her, too, with logical maps,
leave moonprints and material stars,
and return with a handful of eerie dust.

And the helpless sea drags itself
toward her, forever drawn to her tide.
She eyes herself in its mirror, meeting the strange.
As you wake, you may catch her tender reversal,
her act of fading, her partial surrender.

Dividing the Waters

A noise in my head, like liquid thunder complaining
at nothing, at the lack of a home, the need of a moon.
It's the master of repetition, answering a question
with a question, then falling over backwards to make me
change my mind. Shall I embrace flexibility
as the one and only way to get everything I want

such as oceans, waterfalls, staring pools? Want
is one thing, get another. I'm not complaining
but for tides and tears a salty flexibility
is not enough. I must be moody too as a winter moon,
pale-faced with white knuckles, chopping up me
into zillions of us, drowning an answer in a question.

What the straggly sea-mist covers is another question,
one you fret over for years, when what you want
is to walk on water just like me!
Ask yourself, could you ever die without complaining
at the lack of a sign? Or ask affection of the moon
who continually turns her cheek, model of flexibility.

And the waters still teach the unthinkable – flexibility
of l's and m's in a loopy contract. There's no question
about it, you'd do as well to peel the moon
or hitch barefoot round a grain of sand as want
to find the order here. You'd only start complaining
that I'd misled you, that water was behaving only for me.

As if we were separate! The sea is me, as you are me,
as I shall tell you when you're born. A drop of flexibility
has a lot to offer: rephrase your complaining

and it becomes a prayer. Wonder and question,
expect too much and learn by friction. You'll want
to dance or die on another planet, preferably the moon.

What is it arrests the sea daily but my fickle moon,
then drags it groaning back? A short lesson in how to be me:
dry wave, wet desert. What do you want
if not this? There's only one gift, the flexibility
of rivers hurtling towards a final question.
Then there'll be an end to all complaining.

Be eerie like the moon, and athletic. Flexibility
is all, so the waters tell me. And if I may, a question:
diving in like this, don't you want to stop complaining?

Inventing the Fishes

Matter parachutes, free-falls,
takes a tumble. Through this new air
I breed fishes, casting a silver line
for scales, gills, feathery fins.
Here's a rainbow, one of you keep it.

The blue is only as blue as the iris
of a dogfish but powdery, essentially dry.
For now it will do, being open
to suggestions, Friday waiting
to be filled. Clouds fidget when I sigh.

Here's breath, wind, a gale force
to reckon with, shuddering the fluff
of cumulus into fish-bone pleats.
Like sea-sponge they soon puff out,
get together like children,
gather lilacs, make rain.

The horizon maintains a nodding acquaintance,
trying to get used to itself.
Waves too are recent and full of debate,
testing energy against wetness to see
where it leads. The moon's all charged up,
something's up, nothing adds up.
Her reins are not what was promised.

Whales and walruses block the path.
To a stray thread of cloud a starfish
clings. Matter is in hand.
Far, far below the sea mourns
its little fishes, never born, its sonar moan
a chord, like all chords, sliding into
a found divide: urchin, monk, flying sword.

The First Acorn

I polish your sturdy home, humming to myself
as I think of carpenters, boat-builders
and the vast shadowlands of forest.
For company I'll give you elm and ash,
hornbeam and lime, a heritage of spiders
and the mossy truth of a blackbird's nest.

Your old man's skin will bear the troth
of lovers and your heart, pale as sand,
will stretch in ripples as the seasons pass.
A child will lean against your trunk
and feel a world beyond diagrams,
the gravity of purpose in a weighty mass.

And you'll scatter acorns, random hopes,
where they snuffle around in the humus,
fodder for badgers and quivering squirrels.
The few survivors nestle in the loam
where rain and sun and slow design
are, even now, breaking into the house.

Eggshell

I rock fullness in my palm where it hardens
into decision, harking on an oval way of life.
It describes a blue wash, an airy home
that was rinsed in forgetfulness
until it learnt how to be clean.
Well, this is the set of its mind.
Nothing will persuade it
of the delights of softness.

First there is the snowy one,
the cloudy one, a ghost. When you see it
there will be a moment of faintness,
the calm in a kind word:
egg of hawk owl.

Then comes the dun brown, the stone
flecked like a globe with the spent blood
of countries, and with pale promises.
Here the markings of a man falling
or his crisis flung to the wind:
egg of sandpiper.

Centuries will hold them up to the light
and see translucence only, the look
of one who would willingly speak of nothing.

They will sit well
have no entrance
will be eggshell.

Feathers

One, big as a child's fingernail,
will tip its thimbleful of cloud from hedge
to hedge. Others in their proud display
will fix on you unimaginable eyes.
A third nurses a dark secret, fourth
is a lesson in the art of surprise.

All are smooth, reminding you of water
or silk, but their true talent lies
in evasion. See how the air slides off,
as if it's trying to shake hands with snow.

But this is veering off, investing
in the future. For now there's just an arrow
with myriad streamers waxed together
in a flighty alliance: haste, and nerves,
the chasing of the birds.

Butterfly Chapter

One will be flame and charcoal.
My brush seeks the flimsy crêpe
of its wings and paint trembles down.
Once dry, the wings clap shut
as if conferring: I await the verdict.

One will be tiny and boyish,
losing itself against the sky
then appearing like a handful of wishes.
Skittering at eye level, it leaves the air
divided, contemplating a minor tremor.

One is a blank canvas
and gives birth to itself many times over.
It sees no need to kiss the earth.
Instead eyes me from a bed of nettles,
lifts off for a dance with its double.

Lemons are too garish for the next
so I reinvent the meaning of moonlight
and use it to temper its sunny fan.
Now it behaves like a wispy thing,
perfecting the art of leaving.

Grass, Bramble, Herb

Your life will be a pleated one,
given over to slimness.
Dust is not in your nature,
cleanness showing itself in a thin shriek.
Clustering together with your brothers,
you arbitrate the countless shades of green.
How many hooves will pass this way?
Your name is grass.

I give you juice for relentless beaks,
purple that runs with a seaweed pop.
A cowboy's lasso I give you,
and staunch refusal in sappy stalks.
I lay your barbarous cloth over many trunks,
leaving the pins sticking out.
Spiders latch on to you, and childhood's sleeve.
Your name is bramble.

Your leaf will be a grainy wisdom
or an emerald cup; you've a gangly stem
or a flounce of remembered arrows.
I open the aromatic vents, give you
succour's whiff or the sharpness of rind.
In the breeze of my out-breath I hear
a dry violet rattle, a shuffle of seed.
Your name is herb.

The First Poppy

Seeds assemble in a packed house.
From the dark heart I invite
stamens, my only exclamation

then iron out my intentions, crimping
where it suits the grain. Colour
is all. Scraps disintegrate in my hand.

It must be strong, like see-through anger
or pity, an orphan that runs
and runs. Skies offer pink, salmon,
missing the mark. In the wide pupil
of night swarm seeds, drowning.

It will be bold, a statement made
then reiterated, paper-thin
at the mercy of breeze, a fluttering

like that of inadequate wings.
A drop of blood
on my fingers pinpoints mistake.

I stitch the base with sepals,
let tissue film out like a fan.
It crumples as I fumble, slips between
me and my dream. It is my dream.

Pulling away, it bequeaths a trail
of green. My ifs and buts cling on
to dangle as hairs. The stem
is itself, I the one holding.

Cattle, Beasts and Creeping Things

In my box there are tusks and ligaments,
manes and fur. In my box are sleepers and wakers.
I have cackles and grazers and claws in my box.
Honing a delicate heel, I hear thundering
over a free plain, see the dust swirl.

In my box are vertebrates and leaps in the dark.
In my box are the feral and to-be-tamed.
I have suckered feet in my box, and stripes.
Cupping a ribcage, I see liquid skin
take shape, seeping over bone like honey.

In my box a pool of blood, a knock-upon shell.
In my box the whiff of dung, and indelible genes.
Mating calls compete inside my box.
I tailor an eyelid, let the pupil form,
then plant alertness in its waxing void.

In my box the golden brush, the trapper's web.
In my box are snouts, milk and wool.
In my box is the patent black of industry.
I weigh the tonnage of a foot born to wrinkles
and greyness, a concertina of skin.

I have antlers in my box, splitting
like branches or veins. Molars I have,
and whiskers that measure gaps.
Tails flare like the wind's besom,
nostrils steam in rhythmic clouds.

I spread out the contents of my box,
multiples waiting for my guiding hand.
They claim me with innocent and earnest demands.
Uniqueness in mind, I set to work.

Snake

For he will disdain feathers.
For he is devoted to the earth
and rarely leaves her side.

For his tongue splits
and goes about its business.
For his body is a coiled whip.

For in his yielding is power.
For his teeth are fused to the bone.
For he sheds himself of many problems.

For he ingratiates himself with ankles.
For he is not the only one with scales.
For blinking is an unknown pleasure.

For he familiarises himself with exits.
For his insinuations are as the plucking of strings.
For he is dry to the touch, and loves throats.

For he is elongated and limbless.
For his eyes are like wheeling seas.
For his venom is beyond understanding.

For he is about to do his worst.

Wood, Stone, Sand, Clay

I begin with wood: five sappy twigs
that leave a trickle of tears in my palm.
Skimming off the bark, I uncover
their creamy souls – buttermilk,
the surprise of innocent nakedness.
They dry in the sun to brittle bone
and the splinters break off, one by one.

Then stone, smashing one against
the other in a clopping heartbeat.
Despite the sparks, they fail to warm
to my pulse. They are stubborn,
and chafe against the idea of man.
They lie like a row of hunched backs,
where I leave them to the rain's attack.

Sand next, a fistful of lightest earth.
It finds my contours, shifts into place
and matches its warmth to my warmth.
I filter it through my fingers
and listen for the soft landing –
leaf-rustle, or spring showers.
My hand tingles with emptiness.

I find clay, or clay finds me.
It is heavy with longing and rests
its clumpiness against my skin.
Sleep, clay, the sleep of the unborn
and dream of thundering in the blood,
of five senses and an ivory rib,
my sudden breath upon your lips.

SNAIL-WOMAN

Self-contained, yes, and a homemaker,
never one to lift a finger in panic.
Some days she'll sit in her open plan,
labelling jars with that old-maidy stickiness,
head cocked as if hearing for the first time
the blackbird's gift, its tap of shell on flint.

Both hands to the task, she curls herself
around the glass, wavy lettering
attesting the date, the seeming forever
of 1989 giving way to suggestive '0'.
She thought the year could never change,
had already forgotten the previous one,
and the one before, and her astonishment.

For the cabbage leaf is dark and wide,
holds vistas veined enough for any
adventuress, main road running through
like a spine. But for all the holes she makes
she knows, deep down, she's getting nowhere;
a forest of rhubarb and celery intrudes,
kitchen full of apple peel coiled like a world.

One night, when they're all at a standstill
variously snoring or dreaming, closed lids
pulsing out their speed of thought,
she'll creep out into the terrifying moonlight
and thread her bright way, copying Ariadne,
inching off to find herself, or lose it
among the comforting soil, the trunk of arabis,
the smooth mountain she used to call pebble.

BEACHED DOGFISH

Let your palm career along my back,
velvet one way, sandpaper the other.
Corallina I'll call you, your pitying stare,
the drapery of skin, watery flesh and hair.

Aquamarine I propelled myself through
rests in my irises, sinking fast.
You marvel at the colour, so like your own
that Hockney comes to mind, the listless tone

of pools; Atlantic has no time for it,
or for you, or my elemental blue
once a mirror to seaberry, anemone,
clouding fast in a grey disharmony.

My gill's trap-door frets in the wind,
opens and shuts on a pebbled floor.
Find the teeth of my final smile,
tap a nail on its serrated guile

and slide your fingers down my useless fin.
If I shivered with just a spit of life
you'd shrink as from the salt I leave,
shelved by the ocean's wrinkled sleeve.

My every vertebrae sang of shark, morse
in my ear your cruising blood. But net is less
pliant than seaweed; in its chequered sides
I become ancestry, rising against the tide's

magnet to link with an anchored strata
where the sea breeze only half understands
liquidity, and me, in a silver despair,
protesting at suffocation, dryness of air.

ANY OTHER WAY

He hurt me, that's all I can say.
Was fat, and had a funny smell.
Can't put it any other way.

He asked me to come out and play,
said please. I thought I might as well.
He hurt me, that's all I can say.

It was a lovely sunny day.
His buckle clattered like a bell.
Can't put it any other way.

He said it'd all be okay
except he'd kill me if I tell.
He hurt me, that's all I can say.

His eyes were hazel, hair was grey.
He got mad when I tried to yell.
Can't put it any other way.

He said sorry he couldn't stay
then ran off, down to Dingley Dell.
He hurt me, that's all I can say.
Can't put it any other way.

NATURE WALK

Feeling crisp and insubstantial
like ice or breath, I head for the woods.
They're an open door to wintry hints –
bluebell, foxglove, wild garlic shoots,
salmon claws of the early beech.

Leaf-mould and evergreen's different scents
meet halfway, mingling in the drift;
underfoot the pliancy of moss, its limy zest.
Acorn cups give themselves over to emptiness,
brittle as wishbones, a palm of dry wells.

Above's the uneven compass of a January sky,
day slipping through to torch the airy motes
or light the beech's uncertain script.
Steve's carved bravado for Jenny's steamed open
by fifty-four summers, each downward strafe
joining the larger furrow of bark, mottled years.

CATHERINE

Transparent as a leaf that's shed its season
but twice as hopeful, you stand before me
for the sip of wine that makes you girl.

Such tiny sins are bitter-sweet
like a sandal just missing a window,
forget-me-nots huddled together for warmth.

But blue is no answer to your spring iris,
the colour of ambition, horizon's rim.
I say 'just one sip' and shut like the evening,
golden as primroses mirroring your hair.

FEELING THE COLD

The moon is a broken jug I pour myself from,
imitating the flow and coolness of milk.
The wind hasn't finished picking my bones,
neither is the colour of solstice
the dapple-grey mare I had hoped for.

Season folds into season and I still fail
to hold the temperature like a marble
in my pocket. I place its cold curve
on my throat in answer to a vanishing mist,
as if I might make myself transparent too.

Steps on the gravel are like food stored up
for the winter, the cracking of a snail's shell.
I try to ride the sledge of sleep. Marbles roll
down the gulleys of childhood and come to rest.
Their primary colours like flames reach out.

CINDERS

Like the horses I revert to type at midnight,
combing mousey hair. This too was written
in his kiss, my slipper's made-to-measure.

Servants' eyes are discreet but not their whispers;
I'm too easy with them, then sharp when the smell
of polish threatens to take me back. Alone,
I stroke the grain of my chair's buffed arm,
cup its lion's paw in mine as my husband breezes in,
rakish as he feels it his duty to be. He brings news
of our estate like a fresh bouquet – fresh as his collar,
where a vermilion mouth blooms, or as my Two Uglies,
trimmed and pinked.

Newly enslaved, I look for ways to explain myself –
the loneliness of the rich, my absent spouse –
and let sisterhood cloud my thoughts
as the gypsophila this vase, or the hollyhocks the sky,
which I scarcely dare approach.

SLEEPING ON

There is no truth in your book of splinters:
the pages hinge on a faulty recall
of a rusting spinney, timeless gold-leaf.
The sycamore key is long faded, locked
in the humus of a fictional wood.

True, my door is open to the brave:
the deathless spider, more at home than I,
her limp hammock straddling my virgin posts.
Mice soon lose their fear, avoiding only
my breath as they propagate, ransacking
the house as their parents did before them.

But if I can help it, I do not dream.
Brambles know my ways, and comfortable oaks.
And I theirs: the creak of February joints,
the exact angle they allow the wind.
There'll be no gust let through, him in its wake,
no quickening, or sluice-gate lids opening
as the final chapter breathes to a close,
not the look of eyes that have known me or lips
the colour of mine, so recently met.

HANSEL'S BIRTHDAY

Restless in the night, I find you harking back
to the old days of making do, on the hoof.
Dawn is a hunter and you run the gamut,
a fawn who limps his arrowed dream to my lap.

If I told you I'd baked a cake you'd mimic
the lake's transparent smile, make castles vanish
in mid-air like sand running free, running out,
and relive the barley-sugar's matchless kiss.

You were happier then, with berry and shrub,
chafing the plaited rushes of your lead.
Or piping the witch's tune, her five-mile step
no match for my stillness, the coiled entrapment

of a rose. Were we children when I, as swan,
skated the surface of your spilt mind's eye?
Now your fingers dislodge a pebble as white
as a moon or scout's palm your crumbs flew from

and I wear red to match the florist's bundle,
tempting you nearer the party by tugging
your voluminous sleeve, adopted sister,
familiar wife, as full of love as ever.

INSIDE WOLF

I lose a shoe on the way in, as sign – my one
mistake – then teeter on his tongue's root
and dive into cramped air, counting the pillars
of bone that arch and spool like a cocoon.

If I lie flat and stretch out my splayed feet
I can touch his ribs, play the concertina
of their breath. And then I know happiness,
held in a minor key or, as now, drumming thumbs
against the taut and ivory skin of their brow.

His panting chest has me to handle, dead weight
in the adjacent room. I squint straight ahead
but can't decipher one red from another,
untangle threads of satin warp, aortic weft.

And this is as I would have it, though a voice
tunnels from the other side, reassuring me
the hood is intact, that I am alive,
my grandmother too. They have plans
to make me fill his belly with stones,
drag his heavier heart to a glottal stop.

But wolf and me are in this blood bath
together. He arranges knowledge in a swan-song,
music I'll not let him suffer alone.
As womb is grave, I'll not come out
though the gamekeeper and granny
call over my body, each to each.

PERSEPHONE

    1

You call from black soil
I hack and sever from
a winter's torment.

This oak root
though deep enough
only shafts a tunnel
to your blind rising.

I want to know
what is he, the dark one?
Are his teeth as white as
these torn bones
bedded in clay?

His tears, do they
blacken his skin?

My fork scratches
inch by inch.
The ploughshare drags.

Only you can set fire
to frozen earth, green the buds.
Demeter is mad.
Your time is surely come.

2

You don't conceive
the kingdom this is.
Giant attendants
play on my lord.

Their heads are fiery wheels.
They have lost their ears.

Narcissus, yellow as corn,
betrayed me. My lord's carriage, too,
was gold.
Gold as my mother's hair.

They bring no poppies
to sister me. No crown,
no sheaf, no seed of corn

only the bitter mouth
of a pomegranate
round and red as the sun.

Now he watches me waste
to skin that hangs on damp bone.
A dim dream of my mother's pain
vapours in loam.

I do not know
if his teeth are white
for he never smiles
or his tears black
when he sheds none

just looks and grieves
for want of me
to take the seed.

LUCINDA'S ACT

Releasing the faithful trapeze,
rehearsed excuses in her head,
Lucinda Love is ill at ease.

Her sequined partner's hard to please.
Was it something her stand-in said,
releasing the faithful trapeze?

She hopes to God he doesn't freeze;
one slip from him, she's good as dead.
Lucinda Love is ill at ease.

She keeps her gaze above his knees.
Depression weighs her down like lead,
releasing the faithful trapeze.

What he thought real was just a tease;
their balanced poise he took as read.
Lucinda Love is ill at ease.

He's caught a 'cuckold' on the breeze,
remembered last week's unmade bed.
Releasing the faithful trapeze,
Lucinda Love is ill at ease.

BOOKEND

At my back the wordy throng –
soft-spined all,
a paper concertina.

My seahorse head is heavy
rather than highbrow, unshakeable
as it bears the brunt of conquest.

Weighty silence confuses you,
I see reverence grow
in your castaway face

but it's not loneliness
you read in me.

I'm used to separation
from my own kind, the sea
of argument you put between us

as you cultivate
your tousled thoughts,
the little maverick
that rears in you.

My twin and me
have the advantage –
a quiet place to think
a missing torso

and an unchanging view
of a white wall,
an empty page.

Recent Poetry from Anvil

BEI DAO
Old Snow
Translated by Bonnie McDougall & Chen Maiping

NORMAN CAMERON
Collected Poems
AND SELECTED TRANSLATIONS
Edited by Warren Hope & Jonathan Barker

CAROL ANN DUFFY
Mean Time
POETRY BOOK SOCIETY RECOMMENDATION

HARRY GUEST
Coming to Terms

JAMES HARPUR
A Vision of Comets

SARAH KIRSCH
Winter Music
Translated by Margitt Lehbert

MARIUS KOCIEJOWSKI
Doctor Honoris Causa

CHARLES MADGE
Of Love, Time and Places
SELECTED POEMS

DENNIS O'DRISCOLL
Long Story Short

PHILIP SHERRARD
In the Sign of the Rainbow

A catalogue of our publications is available on request